Helping Children See Jesus

ISBN: 978-1-64104-066-2

Christian Growth
New Testament Volume 40:
1 and 2 Peter

Author: Maureen Pruitt, Doris Stuber Moose
Illustrator: Vernon Henkel
Colorization courtesy of Good Life Ministries
Typesetting and Layout: Patricia Pope

© 2019 Bible Visuals International
PO Box 153, Akron, PA 17501-0153
Phone: (717) 859-1131
www.biblevisuals.org

All rights reserved. No part of this publication may be reproduced, stored in a retrieval system or transmitted in any form by any means, electronic, mechanical, photocopy, recording or otherwise, without the prior permission of the publisher, except as provided by USA copyright law.

RELATED ITEMS

To access related items (such as activities, memory verse posters and translated texts) please visit our web store at shop.biblevisuals.org and enter 1040 in the search box on the page.

FREE TEXT DOWNLOAD

To access a FREE printable copy of the teaching text (PDF format) in English or other available languages, enter S1040DL in the search box. Add the item to your cart, and use coupon code XTACSV17 at checkout. Once your order is processed you will receive an email with a link to the free download.

Grow in grace, and in the knowledge of our Lord and Saviour Jesus Christ.

2 Peter 3:18a

Lesson 1
FAITH AND VIRTUE

NOTE TO THE TEACHER

Every book in the Bible is important. Each one contains truths which should affect our lives. (See 2 Timothy 3:16-17.) The letters written by Peter are no exception. From this first epistle we learn how the Christian life develops: (1) It begins with *salvation* (1 Peter 1:1-12). (2) After salvation, the newborn child of God must grow. He must live a pure life because he is set apart by God for Himself. This is *sanctification* (1 Peter 1:13-2:12). (3) *Submission*, one of the important disciplines of Christian living, is next discussed in detail (1 Peter 2:13-3:12). (4) Peter further explains that *suffering* is part of growing up in Christ (1 Peter 3:13-5:14). These truths will be discussed in the first three lessons. We will explore Peter's second letter in the fourth study.

The Christians to whom Peter wrote were scattered and needed encouragement. Many were suffering for their faith in Christ. Their neighbors, perhaps their employers, hated the Gospel which the Christians believed. So the believers were persecuted. False teachers denied the very teachings for which the Christians were suffering. Peter's letters, therefore, brought comfort, hope, and advice to the believers.

In Second Peter 1:5-7, the Holy Spirit lists eight qualities of Christian birth and growth. These are the subjects of this series. Much of Peter's life seems to underline these truths. Therefore, we shall study his life and letters together.

If possible, your students should read aloud the verses referred to in Peter's letters.

Scripture to be studied: 1 Peter 1:1-12; 2 Peter 1:5-8; John 1:35-42

The *aim* of the lesson: To help students understand that in order to become a fully developed Christian, certain qualities must be added to faith.

What your students should *know*: Their faith in Christ will be tested.

What your students should *feel*: A desire to be strong and courageous when testings come.

What your students should *do*:

Unsaved: Turn to Christ for salvation from sin.

Saved: Ask for courage to introduce others to Christ.

Assignments: Read 1 Peter 1:1-12 *every* day until the next meeting. In the margins of their Bibles, mark a cross at each verse that speaks of the blood of Christ or salvation.

Lesson outline (for the teacher's and students' notebooks):

1. There must be faith in Christ before growth (1 Peter 1:2-3, 8-9).
2. Faith in Christ is followed by service (Luke 5:1-11).
3. Faith is tested (Matthew 14:22-33).
4. Virtue must be added to faith (Matthew 16:13-19).

The verse to be memorized:

Grow in grace, and in the knowledge of our Lord and Saviour Jesus Christ. (2 Peter 3:18a)

THE LESSON

Have you ever watched a baby grow? At first he lies in one place. He may move his arms and legs a great deal (especially if he's hungry!). But by himself he never gets anywhere. (*Teacher:* Encourage discussion of a baby's development: reaching for objects, crawling, standing, learning to walk, climbing stairs, running.) A normal child stretches himself. He tries new things. Sometimes he succeeds. Often he fails–and tries again. So he grows and develops.

In the Christian life, there must also be growth and development. A born-again person, who does not grow spiritually, is not a normal Christian. What must a child of God do in order to grow? Will he always succeed? What happens if he fails? Listen carefully!

1. THERE MUST BE FAITH IN CHRIST BEFORE GROWTH
1 Peter 1:2-3, 8-9

Simon lived a long time ago. Like all who have been born into this world, he was a sinner. He was selfish. He was proud and boastful. He used bad language, even swearing sometimes. It was his nature to sin just as it is the nature of a dog to bark.

Simon was a Jew. He, like other Jews, looked forward to the coming of the Messiah–the Anointed One whom God would send to be their King. One day Simon's brother, Andrew, rushed home with important news. "Simon!" Andrew exclaimed. "We have found the Messiah–Christ!" And he offered to take Simon to Him.

Immediately Simon hurried along with his brother, probably asking many questions. (For they had to walk many miles.)

Show Illustration #1

The moment Simon saw Christ, he believed this was indeed the Messiah sent by God. Christ Jesus, who knows all about a person, said, "Your name is Simon. You are going to have a new name: Cephas." (See John 1:42.)

Simon liked his new name. He liked what it means: a *stone*. He, Simon, would be stone-like, firm and strong. And he placed all his trust in this One who came from God.

Simon never forgot that day. Years later he wrote two letters (using his Greek name–"Peter"). In his letters he spoke of Jesus Christ who died, gave His life-blood, and rose from the dead. (See 1 Peter 1:2-3; compare 1:18-21; 2:24; 3:18.) He mentioned that those who truly trust in Christ Jesus receive salvation (1:8-9). Their sins are forgiven. They are saved forever–never to be separated from God.

Meeting Christ the Lord changed everything for Simon. He was born again–born into the family of God. (See 1:23.) He was a Christian (one belonging to Christ). Now he would have to grow as a Christian should.

2. FAITH IN CHRIST IS FOLLOWED BY SERVICE
Luke 5:1-11

When Simon and Andrew returned home, they went back to their fishing business. Did they study the Scriptures to learn more about the Messiah [the Anointed One]? Did they talk about Him, think about Him? They must have. For who could meet Christ and not think and speak of Him?

One morning (probably months later), the fisherman brothers and their partners were cleaning and mending their nets. (See Matthew 4:18-22; Mark 1:16-20; Luke 5:1-11.) To their amazement a great crowd–with Christ in the center–came their way. Jesus turned to Simon and asked, "Will you take me out a little way from the land in your boat?" Simon agreed immediately. Think of it! Simon had God the Son in his very own boat! From the boat the Lord taught all the people who stood on the shore.

Afterward He said, "Simon, go out into the deep water. Let down your *nets* for a catch of fish."

Simon felt it would be a waste of time to fish at this hour of the day. He explained (perhaps not too patiently!), "Master, we fished all night. And we didn't catch a thing." Pausing, he added with a sigh, "But I will let down the *net*."

Casting the *net*, he quickly caught so many fish that his *net* began to break. "Help!" Simon shouted, motioning to the other fishermen. The men scooped hundreds of slippery, floundering fish into both boats. Fish, fish, more fish! So many, that their boats began to sink!

Show Illustration #2

When Simon saw what was happening, he dropped to his knees before Christ. "Go away from me," he prayed. "I am a sinful man. O Lord."

In those few words Simon confessed he was a sinner. He admitted that Christ is the Lord. The Lord Christ heard Simon's prayer. He knew Simon was sorry for his sin. He understood that Simon had faith in Him. So He said, "Simon, do not be afraid. From now on you will fish for men." (This meant he would tell people of Jesus.)

Simon and the others brought their boats to land. And immediately they left everything and followed the Lord. Boats, nets, and fish were no longer important to them. Now they would be disciples–learners of the Great Teacher who chose them for His service.

Years later when Simon wrote his first letter, he may have thought of this day. He knew he was among those whom Christ had chosen (elected) for Himself. (See 1 Peter 1:2; compare John 15:16.) He realized what it meant to give up his fishing business. But he, like all who follow the Lord, would have something far better. He would have a reward that God would keep for him in Heaven forever. And God would keep *him* for that reward. (See 1 Peter 1:4-5.) To "fish for men," as Christ had said, meant he would preach the Gospel. (See 1 Peter 1:25.) He would tell people of the Saviour who rescues them from the darkness of sin and brings them into His own marvelous light. (See 1 Peter 2:9.)

Altogether, the Lord Jesus had many disciple-learners. (See John 6:66.) But in time He chose twelve to be with Him (Mark 3:14). In addition to being disciple-learners, the Lord named them apostles (Matthew 10:2). [An apostle is "one who is sent" to preach.] Now the Lord Jesus called Simon by another name: Peter. (See Matthew 10:2; Mark 3:16; Luke 6:14.)

3. FAITH IS TESTED
Matthew 14:22-33

From the moment that Simon Peter turned to the Lord, he was a man of faith. He gave up his business and by faith followed Christ. During the next months he heard the Lord Jesus preach. He saw Him do many miracles. And Peter's faith kept growing.

One evening Jesus sent the disciples off by boat on Lake Galilee while He went up a mountain to pray. Suddenly a raging storm arose. The disciples' boat bobbed about in the waves. The men rowed with all their strength. Toward morning, aching from tiredness, they saw Someone walking on the lake. Terrified, they cried out, "It's a ghost!"

"Cheer up!" the Walker called. "It is *I*. Do not be afraid!"

Peter thought he recognized the voice. He shouted, "If it is You, Lord, tell me to come to You on the water."

"Come," Jesus commanded.

Peter scrambled out of the boat and walked. He actually walked on the water, heading straight for the Lord Jesus. Peter was delighted! But hearing the howling wind, he turned to see the waves rising higher and higher. In an instant, he began to sink. "Lord, save me!" he cried.

Immediately Jesus reached out His hand and caught Peter.

Show Illustration #3

"O Peter, you have such a little faith. Why did you doubt?" Jesus knew Peter had faith. But He wanted him to have more faith. So He had Peter walk back to the boat with Him! When they were safely in the boat, the wind stopped. And the men worshiped Jesus, saying, "You are truly the Son of God." (Can *you* say that?)

Peter's faith in the Son of God was tested in many ways until the day he died. But the tests made his faith stronger. In one of his letters he wrote that our faith, too, will be tried. (See 1 Peter 1:7; 3:12-17; 4:12-19.) Our bodies may suffer. We may have to do without certain things. Because we are Christians others may make fun of us. But when we accept trials without losing faith in Christ, He is honored now and forever. (Is your life an honor to Him?)

4. VIRTUE MUST BE ADDED TO FAITH
Matthew 16:13-19

Near the end of his life, the Apostle Peter listed seven qualities which must be added to faith in Christ. (Read 2 Peter 1:5-8.) Peter wrote, "Add to your faith, virtue." To have virtue is to be courageous and strong.

Peter believed that Jesus was the Messiah sent from God. He addressed Him as Lord. He worshiped Him as the Son of God. But not many believed and spoke as Peter did.

One day the Lord Jesus gathered together His twelve followers. "Whom do men say that I am?" He asked. (See Matthew 16:13-19; Mark 8:27-29; Luke 9:18-20.)

One replied, "Some say You are John the Baptist" [raised from the dead].

Another answered, "Others say You are Elijah" [returned from Heaven].

"Some think You are Jeremiah or one of the other prophets [who have come back to earth]," said a third.

"But," said Jesus, "whom do *you* say that I am?"

Show Illustration #4

Simon Peter spoke up at once. "You are the Christ, the Son of the living God."

It was not popular to speak out for Christ. The religious leaders could make life hard for Peter. But he was strong and courageous. To *his faith* in Christ, he was adding *virtue*.

What about *you*? Have you placed all your trust in the Lord Jesus Christ? If not, will you do so at this moment? If *you* are a Christian believer, do you tell others of Christ? If not, will you ask Him for courage to speak for Him, so He will not be ashamed of you? (See Matthew 10:32-33.)

Lesson 2
KNOWLEDGE AND SELF-CONTROL

Scripture to be studied: 1 Peter 1:13-2:12

The *aim* of the lesson: To enable the students to see the necessity of growing in spiritual knowledge and self-control.

What your students should *know*: Their decisions and actions should be determined by the teaching of the Word of God.

What your students should *feel*: A longing to have their manner of living and their speech controlled by the Spirit of God.

What your students should *do*: Turn at once from unholy living and uncontrolled speaking.

Assignment: Read *daily* 1 Peter 1:13-2:12. Underline the word *holy* wherever it appears.

Lesson outline (for the teacher's and students' notebooks):

1. Children of God must have knowledge (Matthew 16:21; Mark 8:31; Luke 9:22; 19:10; John 2:19-22; 1 Peter 1:13-14).
2. Mature knowledge of God leads to holy living (Matthew 17:1-8; Mark 9:2-13; Luke 9:28-36; 1 Peter 1:15-16).
3. Holy living is normal for the growing Christian (Matthew 17:24-27; 18:21-35; 19:27-30; Mark 10:28-31; Luke 18:28).
4. Add to knowledge, self-control (John 13:3-17).

The verse to be memorized:

Grow in grace, and in the knowledge of our Lord and Saviour Jesus Christ. (2 Peter 3:18a)

NOTE TO THE TEACHER

The moment a person is born into the family of God, he is sanctified. That is, he is set apart by God for Himself. (You may wish to refer to NT Volume 21 which deals with *Sanctification*.) In Peter's first letter he refers to this subject (1:13-2:12). God who is holy, wants His children to live holy lives. ("Holy," "saint," and "sanctified," all mean the same.) The more we know about God and His Son (and what They have done for us), the more we should long to be holy in our conduct.

THE LESSON

Have you ever said something you were sorry for? The minute the words were out of your mouth, you thought, *Why did I say such a thing*? Maybe you spoke without knowing all the facts. Or perhaps you were puffed up and tried to impress others. (*Teacher:* Mention something you yourself said thoughtlessly. Encourage students to share their experiences.) Unfortunately, once you had said it, you could not call it back.

Simon Peter said many good things, some of which we learned in our last lesson. (Have students mention what Peter said.) There were times, however, when Peter wished he could take back certain words. He may have been thinking of some of those words when the Holy Spirit caused him to write, " . . . Giving all diligence [earnest care], add to your faith, virtue; and to virtue, knowledge; and to knowledge, self-control" (2 Peter 1:5-6). Peter needed knowledge so he would know what to say. He also needed self-control to be kept from saying things he should not say.

1. CHILDREN OF GOD MUST HAVE KNOWLEDGE
Matthew 16:21; Mark 8:31; Luke 9:22, 19:10; John 2:19-22; 1 Peter 1:13-14

Peter and the other disciples were to have only three years with the Son of God. And He had so much to teach them!

One day the Lord Jesus spoke of Himself plainly saying, "The Son of Man must suffer many things . . . He will be killed, and after three days rise again." (See Matthew 16:21; Mark 8:31; Luke 9:22.) But these were truths the disciples didn't understand. (See John 2:19-22.) They believed that Jesus, the Messiah sent from God, would be King. Surely their *King* wouldn't suffer and die!

Peter told the Lord, "This won't happen to You!"

Show Illustration #5

Jesus answered sharply, "Get behind Me, Satan! You don't understand the plan of God."

Think of it! Peter had spoken for Satan. Why? Because he didn't understand what God had planned.

Years later the Spirit of God said through Peter, "Think seriously and thoughtfully . . . Do not . . . speak as you used to do when you were ignorant and did not know any better." (See 1 Peter 1:13-14.)

Peter needed knowledge. He had to learn the plans of God and speak wisely.

2. MATURE KNOWLEDGE OF GOD LEADS TO HOLY LIVING
Matthew 17:1-8; Mark 9:2-13; Luke 9:28-36; 1 Peter 1:15-16

Shortly after speaking so sternly to Peter, the Lord Jesus took him and James and John up into a high mountain. There Jesus prayed. And the three disciples fell asleep. (See Luke 9:32.) Suddenly the face of the Lord shone as the sun. His clothing glistened. He was completely changed. Amazingly, two brightly shining men appeared from Heaven and talked with Christ. And, of all things, they spoke of His coming death!

At that moment, Peter and the others woke up. Seeing the Lord and the two men all aglow, they were terrified. Peter didn't know what to say. (See Mark 9:6.) Nor did he understand the meaning of what he saw. "Master," he said, "it is good for us to be here. If You are willing, let us build three booths; one for You, and one for each of the two from Heaven."

Show Illustration #6

Immediately Peter knew he should have kept quiet! For a voice–the voice of God Himself–spoke from Heaven. "This is the Son of My love. Listen to *Him*!" Poor Peter. He had so much to learn! No wonder the Spirit of God caused him to write, "Add to your virtue, knowledge." He spoke with courage. But he had spoken without knowledge.

Peter always remembered the day when he saw the Lord in His glittering brightness. Near the close of his life, he wrote, " . . . With our eyes we saw His Majesty, the Lord Jesus Christ. He received from God the Father honor and glory. For there came a voice to Him saying, 'This is the Son of My love, in whom I am well pleased.' And we heard this voice which came from Heaven when we were with Him on the holy mountain." (See 2 Peter 1:16-18.)

To Peter, the mountain was "holy"–a place set apart by God. For it was there he had seen the holy Son of God in His bright, shining glory. He had heard God, the holy One, speak. Later Peter was prompted by God's Spirit to write of holiness, saying, "As He who has called you is holy, so you are to be holy in all your living. God has written [in the Old Testament Scriptures], 'You must be holy because I am holy'." (See 1 Peter 1:15-16; Leviticus 11:44.) Now Peter understood that God sets apart [sanctifies, makes holy] His own people for Himself. In turn, they are to live lives and speak words that are holy, pure, and good. (Read 1 Peter 2:21-23.)

3. HOLY LIVING IS NORMAL FOR THE GROWING CHRISTIAN
Matthew 17:24-27; 18:21-35; 19:27-30; Mark 10:28-31; Luke 18:28

Peter wanted to grow as a Christian should. He wanted to live a holy life–one which honored God. But he had questions. For example, did God the Son have to pay taxes for the work of His own house (the temple)? Should he, Peter, a servant of God, pay this tax?

The Lord Jesus explained that tax collectors and others did not accept Him as the Son of God. If He refused to pay the tax, they would be so offended that they might never trust in Him.

Show Illustration #7

So Jesus said, "You go down to the lake, Peter. Throw in a hook and line. Look in the mouth of the first fish you catch. In it you will find a piece of money. Use that to pay the tax for both of us." Imagine! The *right* amount in a fish's mouth–the first fish, too! (See Matthew 17:24-27.) Peter's question was answered. Just as the Lord Jesus paid taxes, so Peter was to pay taxes.

There was something else Peter wanted to know. He asked, "Lord, how often am I to forgive my brother who sins against me? Seven times?"

"No," Jesus answered, "not seven times; but 70 times seven." (*Teacher:* have students figure out 70 x 7.)

Peter could hardly believe what he heard. The Lord Jesus was actually telling him to keep on and on forgiving. *How* could he forgive another so many times? *Why* should he do so? Knowing his thoughts, Jesus told him this story.

A servant owed the king a great amount of money. The king demanded that the servant pay back his debt. "O king!" the servant cried, "I cannot pay you for I have no money."

The king commanded his men, "Sell him as a slave! Sell his wife and children! Sell everything he has! I want that money!"

The servant fell before the king begging, "Oh, be patient with me, your Majesty. I will pay you back everything I owe."

That touched the king. "Set him free!" he ordered. "I forgive him. He doesn't have to repay me."

The servant rushed home to tell his wife the good news. On the way, he met a man who owed him a tiny little bit. He grabbed the man by the throat, shouting, "Pay me back the money you owe!"

"Wait a little longer and I'll pay you everything," the man promised.

"No! I will not wait." And he had the man thrown into prison!

Some who saw what happened, reported to the king.

The king called the man whom he had forgiven. "You wicked servant!" he exclaimed. "I forgave you your large debt. You should have had pity on that man as I had on you. Now you must pay back all you owe!" And he tossed his servant into jail.

Hearing this story, Peter began to understand what Jesus had been teaching. As God forgives our sins–our many, many sins–so we ought to forgive the few wrong things that others do to us, or the wrongs we *imagine* they do.

Peter's knowledge was growing. (1) Like everyone else, he, a servant of the Lord, had to pay taxes. (2) A child of God forgives those who sin against him–and keeps on forgiving and forgiving and forgiving. (See Ephesians 4:32.) This is part of what it means to live a holy, normal, growing Christian life.

Did Peter think of these truths later when he wrote, "You are chosen and set apart–a people for God's special possession?" Therefore, "You should show to others the excellencies of Him who has called you out of darkness into His marvelous light." (See 1 Peter 2:9.)

4. ADD TO KNOWLEDGE SELF-CONTROL
John 13:3-17

Shortly before the Lord Jesus died, Peter learned another lesson. And again he spoke when he should have been quiet.

Show Illustration #8

Christ and the Twelve had gathered to eat their last Passover meal together. Since it was a borrowed room, there was no host to wash their feet. So Jesus tied a towel around Himself, and going from one to another, He washed the feet of each disciple. This was the work of a slave. Peter, watching, was stunned. Pulling his feet under him, he exclaimed, "Lord, are *You* [the holy One] going to wash *my* feet? No! [I am too sinful.] *You* can never wash *my* feet."

Patiently, kindly, Jesus answered, "If *I* do not wash you, *you* have no part [no fellowship] with Me."

Quickly Peter declared, "Lord, do not wash only my feet. Wash my hands and my head also. Give me a bath all over!"

Jesus replied, "Anyone who has bathed his body needs only to wash his feet. Then he is clean all over."

After He finished washing their feet, Jesus sat down. Looking searchingly at the men, he asked, "Do you understand what I have done? You call Me Master and Lord. That is good. For so I am. Therefore, since I, your Lord and Master, have washed your feet, you also should wash one another's feet. I have given you an example. You should do as I have done. I tell you, the servant is not greater than his Lord . . . If you know these things, you are happy if you do them." (See John 13:3-17.)

Years later Peter would have remembered the lesson Christ Jesus taught that night. The Spirit of God wrote through Peter: ". . .All of you should serve each other humbly. God resists the proud. He gives grace to the humble. Humble yourselves under the mighty hand of God, so He may honor you." (See 1 Peter 5:6.)

Peter had many things to learn. With his knowledge, he needed self-control. We, too, need to add these qualities to our daily lives. If you're a child of God, is it clear to you that God has sanctified you–set you apart for Himself? You are holy. In turn, are you living a holy life that pleases Him? Are you a truly humble servant of the Lord God? Do you help others as a slave would help his master? Have you learned when to speak–and when *not* to speak?

Think seriously now. Are you truly adding to your faith, virtue; to virtue, knowledge; and to knowledge, self-control?

Lesson 3
PATIENCE AND GODLINESS

NOTE TO THE TEACHER

As we have seen in the first two lessons, in Peter's first letter the Holy Spirit deals with: (1) Salvation, 1:1-12 and (2) Sanctification, 1:13-2:13.

Two other subjects in the epistle (which are discussed in this lesson) are: (3) Submission, 2:13-3:12 and (4) Suffering, 3:13-5:14.

To be submissive to another, takes patience (endurance). So it is not surprising that the Spirit of God commands us to add patience to self-control. To patience is to be added godliness. (See 2 Peter 1:6.) Is our love for God true and pure? Does He have our loyal devotion? What we really *are* is often revealed through suffering. For many, Godlikeness comes as a *result* of suffering.

The opening question in today's lesson should be addressed to your particular group. If you are teaching children and young people, encourage them to discuss how they should feel and act toward those who are older. (See 1 Peter 3:8-12; 5:5-6.) Ask working people what God requires in the servant-master relationship. (See 1 Peter 2:18-20; 3:8-12.) While masters are not mentioned directly in First Peter, they too should consider their duties. (See Colossians 4:1.) Wives should speak of the Biblical teaching regarding their attitudes toward their husbands. (See 1 Peter 3:1-6, 8-12.) Husbands ought to talk about their responsibilities to their wives. (See 1 Peter 3:7, 8-12.) All groups should see the need for obeying the laws of the land. (See 1 Peter 2:13-17; 3:8-12.) Stress that *all* are to be submissive to others. (See 1 Peter 5:5.)

Scripture to be studied: 1 Peter 2:13-5:14

The *aim* of the lesson: To encourage students to be fearless in their Christian witness.

  What your students should *know*: Christians must submit to others.

  What your students should *feel*: A desire to be patient and God-like in every situation.

  What your students should *do*: Determine what they can do this week to improve their Christian growth.

Assignment: Read 1 Peter 2:13-3:12, listing in their notebooks those who are to be submissive, whom they are to serve, and why.

Lesson outline (for the teacher's and students' notebooks):
1. Christians need to be patient (1 Peter 2:22-23).
2. Christians must wait patiently for the Lord (Psalm 37:7; John 21:1-14; James 5:7-11).
3. God uses people who are God-like (Acts 1:12-26; 2:1-41).
4. Godliness may lead to suffering (1 Peter 5:10).

The verse to be memorized:

Grow in grace, and in the knowledge of our Lord and Saviour Jesus Christ. (2 Peter 3:18a)

THE LESSON

Do you find it easy to obey those who are in authority over you? In Peter's first letter, God gives commands to everyone: children, young people, servants, husbands, wives, citizens. All are to yield to and obey those who are over them. When people follow God's rules, He blesses them with happiness. Those who disobey His commands cannot be happy–and usually make those around them unhappy!

We have already seen that to grow in the Christian life we are to add to our faith, virtue (courage); to virtue, knowledge; and to knowledge, self-control. Two more qualities are mentioned: patience and godliness (2 Peter 1:6). These are especially needed since we are to give in to those who are over us.

1. CHRISTIANS NEED TO BE PATIENT
1 Peter 2:22-23

The evening before the Lord Jesus died, He talked with His disciples. "Tonight," He said, "you will all run off and leave Me."

Peter said, confidently, "All the others may run away. But *I* will never leave You!"

Jesus warned, "Peter, before morning comes, three times you will have told people you don't even know Me."

Peter replied even more certainly, "Though I should die with You, I will not deny You." (See Matthew 26:33-35; Mark 14:29-31; Luke 22:31-34; John 13:36-38.)

Later, in the Garden of Gethsemane, the Lord Jesus took Peter, James and John apart from the other disciples. "You wait here," He told the three. "While you wait, pray, so you will not yield to temptation."

Leaving them, Jesus prayed alone. They should have obeyed the Lord. Instead, they went to sleep.

When the Lord Jesus awakened them, they were terrified. "Look!" He said. "Here is the one [Judas] who is betraying Me into the hands of the enemy."

Blinking awake, the disciples reached for their swords. "Master, shall we fight?" they asked.

Show Illustration #9

Peter didn't wait for an answer. He whipped out his sword and slashed about with it. Off came the ear of the servant of the high priest! Immediately Jesus replaced the ear. And He scolded Peter–Peter, who had been too impatient to hear what the Lord wanted him to do.

Then Jesus, God the Son, Creator of Heaven and earth, allowed His enemies to lead Him away as a common prisoner. Through the night they took Him from one place to another. Patiently He answered many questions asked by the Jewish religious leaders and Roman governors.

At the same time, Peter was also answering questions. "Are you one of Jesus' disciples?" A young girl asked. (See John 18:17.)

Loudly enough for all to hear, Peter lied, saying, "I am not!"

Later, someone else asked, "Are you one of His disciples?"

With an oath Peter shouted, "I am not!"

Another said, "Didn't I see you in the garden with Jesus?"

"I do not know the Man!" Peter snorted, cursing and swearing. And at that moment he saw the Lord looking at him.

Peter's virtue (courage) had failed. He had no patience, no godliness. He would remember that awful night years afterward when God's Spirit wrote through him: ". . .Christ. . .suffered for us, leaving us an example, that you should follow His steps. He never sinned. No bad talk or lies came from His mouth. When people spoke against Him, He did not talk back. (See 1 Peter 2:21-23.) And, "If you want a joyful, happy life, do not say bad things." (See 1 Peter 3:10.)

2. CHRISTIANS MUST WAIT PATIENTLY FOR THE LORD
Psalm 37:7; John 21:1-14; James 5:7-11

After denying the Lord, Peter went out and wept bitterly. (See Matthew 26:75; Luke 22:62.) Soon Christ was dead. Peter's days and nights blurred into one.

On Sunday morning, a woman came rushing to Peter and John with bad news. "They have taken away the Lord out of the tomb. We do not know where they have laid Him!"

The two men raced to the garden, entered the empty tomb, and saw the linen grave clothes. But Jesus' body was not in the wrappings! They couldn't understand it. (See John 20:9.) Sadly they went home.

Soon the women came with good news. "We have seen the Lord. He is alive! He said you are to go to Galilee. He will see you there." (See Matthew 28:8-10.)

Afterwards the Lord went to Peter, too. (See Luke 24:34; 1 Corinthians 15:5.) Was Peter embarrassed? Ashamed? Did he say he was sorry? Shortly, Peter and some of the other disciples went to Galilee. It was a long, long walk (probably 70 miles or more!). There, near Galilee Lake, they waited for the Lord. But Peter was restless. He saw boats and nets and men fishing. He had left all these more than three years before to become a fisher of men. Since he had denied the Son of God, was he useless to Him? Should he go back to his old fishing business?

Finally he announced, "I'm going fishing." He was too impatient to wait for the Lord.

The other disciples decided, "We'll go with you." Off they went in a boat, fished all night–and caught nothing! (See John 21:1-3.)

Show Illustration #10

The next morning, rowing wearily toward shore, they heard Someone calling. "Do you have any fish?"

Unhappily, they answered, "No."

"Cast your net on the right side of the ship, and you will catch fish!" the man promised.

They did. And they caught so many fish they could scarcely pull in the net! "It is the Lord!" John exclaimed.

When Peter heard that, he jumped into the lake and swam to shore, leaving the others to drag the fish-filled net.

On the beach, breakfast was ready and waiting for them. Jesus, Son of God, had cooked a meal. There He served all of them–even Peter.

3. GOD USES PEOPLE WHO ARE GOD-LIKE
Acts 1:12-26; 2:1-41

Some days later the Lord Jesus had His disciples with Him just outside the city of Jerusalem. He commanded them, "Do not leave Jerusalem until the Holy Spirit comes. Wait for Him. He will give you power to speak of Me." (See Acts 1:4-5, 8.) Then, before their very eyes, He ascended to the Father in Heaven.

Day after day passed. The disciples waited. But nothing happened. Was Peter impatient now? Did he think of fishing? No! He was with some others (about 120 altogether). They were praying and Peter was in charge of the group! (See Acts 1:12-26.) To his patience he was adding godliness.

Right on time the Holy Spirit came. And crowds of people were amazed to hear, in their own languages, the mighty works of God. (See Acts 2:1-12.)

Show Illustration #11

Some, however, criticized. So Peter jumped up, shouting, ". . . Listen to me!" Then he clearly explained that God the Son had come to earth. According to the plan of God, He died and rose again. It was a powerful sermon. He ended with, ". . . God has made this same Jesus, *whom you have crucified*, both Lord and Christ. He is the promised One sent from God." (See Acts 2:13-36.)

The people were stunned by Peter's message. "What shall we do?" they demanded.

Peter answered, "Repent, every one of you. Change your mind about Jesus. He is not merely the son of a carpenter. He is the Son of the living God. Receive Him, the Lord from Heaven. Change your manner of life. When you repent, your sins will be forgiven. Having received forgiveness of sin, you must be baptized. This will show to all that you are for Christ the Lord." (See Acts 2:37-41.)

That very day about 3,000 people placed their trust in the Lord Jesus and were baptized! Peter was no longer ashamed of the One who bore "our sins in His own body on the cross." (See 1 Peter 2:24; compare Acts 3:13-15; 4:11; 5:30-31, 41-42.)

4. GODLINESS MAY LEAD TO SUFFERING
1 Peter 5:10

From that time on, Peter preached boldly and fearlessly.

The religious leaders hated Christ. So they commanded, "Do not speak at all nor teach in the name of Jesus."

Peter knew the laws. He knew it was right to obey the leaders. But he knew also that God is above the leaders. Twice Peter explained, "We have to obey God [who has told us to preach]. We dare not disobey Him by obeying men." (See Acts 4:13-20; 5:17-29.)

Show Illustration #12

The leaders were furious! They ordered beatings for Peter and the other apostles. Again they demanded, "Do not speak in the name of Jesus." Then they let them go.

And Peter and the others went out, "rejoicing because they were counted worthy to suffer shame for His name. And each day…they continually taught the people, preaching about Jesus Christ." (See Acts 5:40-42; compare 1 Peter 3:14-18; 4:12-13, 16; 5:10.)

Years later Peter wrote to others who were suffering for speaking of the Lord Christ. He reminded them (and us!) that Christians must obey those who govern the land. (See 1 Peter 2:13-23.) He gave three reasons for doing so: (1) God has planned that rulers are to govern people. (Compare Romans 13:1.) (2) It is God's will that Christians should obey the government. Not to do so, would cause unbelievers to speak against the Lord. (3) During His years on earth, Christ Jesus obeyed those who governed the land.

Peter added, however, that Christians are *servants of God*. (See 1 Peter 2:16.) If the government should order a person to do something against the Lord, then the believer must obey God. Otherwise, the child of God must always obey the laws of the land.

Are you living the kind of life that pleases God? Do you gladly submit to those who have authority over you? Are you known for your patience and God-likeness? Has God spoken to you today about some things that need changing in your life? If so, list them in your notebook. Determine what you can do this week to make those changes. Write these ideas in your notebook.

Now we shall ask the Lord to help you correct your faults. Then will you ask Him to make you a good witness for Him–even if it involves suffering?

Lesson 4
BROTHERLY KINDNESS AND LOVE

Scripture to be studied: 2 Peter 1:1-3:18

The *aim* of the lesson: To teach that we grow *in* our Christian lives according to our knowledge of the Lord.

What your students should *know*: God will reward us according to our growth in grace and knowledge of Christ.

What your students should *feel*: A keen desire to be kind to others and show love in every situation.

What your students should *do*: Determine *to whom* and *how* they will show their kindness and love.

Lesson outline (for the teacher's and students' notebooks):
1. Christians must improve their spiritual lives (2 Peter 1:1-21; Acts 5:1-11).
2. Christians must beware of false teachers (2 Peter 2:1-22; Acts 8:4-24).
3. Christ's coming and brotherly kindness (2 Peter 3:1-13; Acts 10:38-43).
4. Christians must grow in grace and knowledge of Christ (2 Peter 3:14-18; Galatians 2:11-14).

NOTE TO THE TEACHER

In 2 Peter, believers are reminded that they are "partakers of the divine nature" (2 Peter 1:4). After that, the Christian life is a matter of addition. (See 2 Peter 1:5-7.) It is one thing to start well in the Christian life. It is something else to finish well. God wants His own to have a full reward when they get to their heavenly home.

The Lord Jesus had said that for His sake, Peter would die. (See John 13:36, 21:18-19.) And he did, shortly after this letter was written. (See 2 Peter 1:14.)

The verse to be memorized:

Grow in grace, and in the knowledge of our Lord and Saviour Jesus Christ. (2 Peter 3:18a)

THE LESSON

1. CHRISTIANS MUST IMPROVE THEIR SPIRITUAL LIVES
2 Peter 1:1-21; Acts 5:1-11

If you were going to receive a reward, would you rather have a mouthful of rice or a bowlful? (*Teacher:* Name something your students would really like to have. For example: a piece of tortilla or a whole one; a spoonful or dish full of ice cream; an old motorbike or a new one.)

In Peter's last letter, God says He wants all who truly trust in Him to have a big, BIG reward when they get to Heaven. (See 2 Peter 1:11.) He tells too, how all Christian believers can be rewarded. "Do everything you possibly can to live a good Christian life. You have placed your trust in Christ. Now add to your faith, courage, knowledge, self-control, patience, godliness, brotherly kindness and love. If these things overflow from your life, you will be busy. You will have a good knowledge of our Lord Jesus Christ . . . If you are adding these qualities, you will be kept from stumbling into sin. And you will have an abundant reward in Heaven." (See 2 Peter 1:5-11.)

Peter did not have much longer to live when the Spirit of God breathed these words through him. Looking back over his life, he knew there were times when he had not added courage [virtue] to his Christian faith. More than once he had lacked knowledge, not knowing the plan of God. Without self-control, he spoke words he should not have said. He had been impatient. He was not always Godlike. (*Teacher:* allow students to discuss details of Peter's failures.) Now in his old age, Peter probably remembered others who had also stumbled.

Ananias and Sapphira–a married couple–could have been in his thoughts. These two wanted to be praised for doing some good deed. Together they decided to sell part of their land and give money for the work of God. They would let Peter and the other apostles *think* they had given *all* the money. Instead, they would keep some for themselves. This is exactly what they did.

When Ananias brought the money, Peter was displeased. He had no praise for the giver or the gift. Instead Peter asked, "Ananias, why has Satan filled your heart to lie to the Holy Spirit, and to keep back part of the price of the land?"

Show Illustration #13

Ananias was shocked. How could Peter know about the money he left at home?

Peter continued, "Before you sold your land it belonged to you. After you sold it, you could have done what you wanted with the money. Why did you decide to make it appear *as if* you brought *all* the money? You have lied to God, not to men."

At that very moment, Ananias fell to the ground dead. God had punished him.

About three hours later Sapphira came to Peter. She doubtless expected to hear the people praise her for the gift her husband had brought.

"Tell me," Peter said to her, "did you sell the land for *this* amount of money?"

"Yes," Sapphira answered boldly. "We sold the land for the amount we have given you."

Peter said sternly, "Why did you and your husband agree to lie to the Spirit of the Lord? The men who have buried your husband are just outside the door. They will bury you also."

And Sapphira, having lied to God, also dropped dead. God had wanted her and her husband to add good qualities to their lives. He wanted to reward them for giving to Him. But how could He? They had been dishonest. What a pity!

2. CHRISTIANS MUST BEWARE OF FALSE TEACHERS
2 Peter 2:1-22; Acts 8:4-24

Peter, knowing he would soon die (see 2 Peter 1:14), was concerned for all Christians. He wanted to warn them (and us!) against any teaching that would lead them away from God. He explained in his letter that there had been people who had prophesied falsely long ago. (See Jeremiah 14:14; 27:10; Ezekiel 13:3-4.) In the same way, he said, there would also be false teachers in the Church. They would come in secretly, bringing teaching that would destroy those who accepted it. They would even deny the Lord who had bought them with His life-blood! (See 2 Peter 2:1.) These false teachers would be covetous–that is, they would want for themselves what belonged to others. (See 2 Peter 2:3, 14.) They would speak proudly, getting honor for themselves. (See 2 Peter 2:18.)

As Peter wrote this message from God, would he have thought of a man he had met in Samaria years before? Perhaps.

This man, named Simon, was famous for the amazing things he could do through his powers of magic. Many listened to him and followed him, thinking he must be from God. One day, Philip (a true disciple of our Lord) came to Samaria, preaching about Jesus Christ. Never had the people heard such words as his. Nor had they ever seen the kinds of miracles he did. Demon-possessed men and women were set free from tormenting evil spirits. The sick and lame were healed. Hearing and seeing Philip, many believed on Jesus Christ as Saviour. And they let it be known to all by being baptized.

When Simon saw the amazing miracles, he knew that Philip had greater power than he did. So he asked to be baptized.

Meanwhile, Peter and John heard about Philip's work in Samaria. So they came from Jerusalem to help him. Laying their hands on the new believers, they prayed for them. And the Holy Spirit came upon them.

Simon, seeing this, was more amazed than ever. If he could have the same power as these disciples, he would indeed be a very popular man.

So he went to Peter secretly, saying, "I will give you money for this power which you have. Will you sell it to me so anyone on whom I place my hands may receive the Holy Spirit?"

Show Illustration #14

Peter answered fiercely, "How dare you think that the gift of God can be bought with money! Your heart isn't honest in the sight of God. Turn from this great wickedness. Pray that the Lord will forgive the thoughts of your heart. You are bound by your own sin."

Simon answered, "Pray for me so nothing will happen to me." He did not ask for forgiveness. He simply wanted to escape punishment.

Peter in his letter, warned that false teachers will certainly be judged. There is no escape for them, just as there was none for sinning angels, men or cities. (See 2 Peter 2:1, 4-9.) There will always be false teachers. But children of God are to turn away from them.

3. CHRIST'S COMING AND BROTHERLY KINDNESS
2 Peter 3:1-13; Acts 10:38-43

Near the end of his letter, Peter wrote of the return to earth of the Lord Jesus. (See 2 Peter 3:1-11.) This was a truth he loved. (See 1 Peter 1:7, 10-13; 4:13; 5:4.) He warns, however, that before Christ comes, many will laugh at the idea. "What happened to the promise of His coming?" they will ask.

Peter answers, "God and men measure time differently. To God, a thousand years is as only one day. God will keep His promise. Christ will come to earth again. The reason for the delay is this: God does not want anyone to perish and be separated from Him forever. He wants *everyone* to turn to the Saviour." (See 2 Peter 3:9.)

Years before, this truth had not been clear to Peter. He thought the Gospel message was only for some very special people: the Jews. (Peter himself was Jewish.) God had to speak to him through a vision to show him he was wrong. (*Teacher:* This experience from Peter's life is given in detail in *Conversion*, Volume 17 of this series.) At that time it was not easy for Peter to obey God. (See Acts 10:1–11:18.) To witness to the hated Gentiles would take kindness–brotherly kindness. And Peter added this quality to his spiritual life.

Show Illustration #15

He preached exactly the same message to the non-Jews as he had preached to the Jews. That is, Christ proved by His life that He is the Son of God; He was crucified; He was raised from the dead; He is the Judge of all. Then Peter invited the Gentiles to place their trust in Christ and receive forgiveness of sins. And many turned at once to the Lord. (See Acts 10:38-43.)

Is there someone somewhere–or a group of people anywhere–who should hear the Gospel from your lips? Have you refused to take the message of God because you do not like him (or them)? If so, you need brotherly kindness. Are you willing to add this quality to your life?

4. CHRISTIANS MUST GROW IN GRACE AND KNOWLEDGE OF CHRIST
2 Peter 3:14-18; Galatians 2:11-14

According to the list in Peter's letter, Christians by their lives must also show what love is. This is not always easy. But it is possible, as Peter himself proved. He had once decided that the Gentile Christians ought also to follow certain Jewish rules.

Show Illustration #16

When the Apostle Paul, who had turned to Christ long after Peter had, heard this, he spoke sternly to Peter. And he did it in public! (See Galatians 2:11-14.)

Was Peter embarrassed? What did he say? There's no record that he said anything. He, the great leader of the first church, had been wrong. He even bowed to one younger than himself. Indeed, near the end of his letter, he spoke of the wisdom of his "beloved brother Paul." (See 2 Peter 3:15.) Peter added love to his spiritual life.

His last written words are those of our memory verse: " . . . Grow in grace, and in the knowledge of our Lord and Saviour Jesus Christ . . . " Growing and knowing go together. For we can only grow spiritually as we learn to know the Lord. (Compare 2 Peter 1:8.) The more earnestly [diligently] we seek to know Him and to grow in His likeness, the greater will be our reward when we see Him. (See 2 Peter 1:5, 10-11; 3:14.)

Will you write in your notebook exactly how you want to improve your spiritual life this week? To whom can you show brotherly kindness? How can you show love for someone else? How do you plan to learn more about Christ Jesus the Lord?

www.ingramcontent.com/pod-product-compliance
Lightning Source LLC
Chambersburg PA
CBHW060803090426
42736CB00002B/136